Disgruntled or Over-Medicated?

A Profile of Joseph Wesbecker

by P.O. Doe

About the author

P.O. Doe is a Probation Officer working in a major metropolitan area in the United States. He needs to remain anonymous due to privacy concerns and politics in the workplace. He has been working with the same agency for over a decade and has worked in many different assignments within the department. He holds several college degrees, a requirement for most Probation Officer positions. He lives with his wife and family in a city a good distance away from where he works.

Copyright P. O. Doe 2018

Contents

Behavioral Background

General Characteristics of a Profile:

There are some basic factors that make up a profile. In the makeup of a mass murder offender, the exact etiology is unclear. It is the unique combination of the biology, the sociology, and the personal psychology of an individual, which accounts for the personality and thus the behavior of an individual[9]. But in their actions, there appears to be some basic similarities within the typologies. The five typologies used here for mass murder are the Family Annihilator, the Pseudo Commando, the Disgruntled Employee, the Disciple and the Set-and-Run Killer.

Some factors that are generally addressed in a profile are age, gender, race, motivation, anticipated gain, intelligence, spatial mobility, victim traits, victim relationship, and victim selectivity. Other factors to consider are precursor behavior or events, firearm ownership, abuse history and suicidal inclinations.

Factors such as age, gender, intelligence and race need no further definition. Motivation is what drives the killer and is divided into two basic types: intrinsic or extrinsic. Anticipated gain is what the person is expected to realize as an end to his actions, and is divided into psychological or material gain. Spatial mobility is the killer's proclivity to travel from their area of origin, and is divided into geographically stable or geographically transient. Victim traits are characteristics that the victims have in common, such as hair color or race. Victim selectivity is how the victim is chosen, and is divided into random and nonrandom. Victim relationship is how the killer knows the victim's, and is divided into affiliate and stranger[9]. Precursor behaviors or events are those that lead up to the event or trigger the event, such as loss of a job, relationship problems or talking about committing the crime long before hand. Firearm ownership refers to recent purchase of firearms or possible an obsession with them. Abuse history concerns the killers past history of being physically, sexually, verbally or psychologically abused or the killer's history of abusing animals or other people. The suicidal inclinations refer to the killer's will or plan to die[2].

Profile: Age

The age of the offender is different within the breakdown of type. Douglas and Olshaker[4] put the overall age as mid to late 30's to mid to late 40's. Yet when describing a Pseudo-Commando or assassin personality type of mass murderer, Douglas and Olshaker[4] state that the normal activation time for the event is in the offender's late 20's. Mendoza[14] describes the age of a mass murderer offender as young, without being more specific to numbers. Fessenden's[6] study of rampage killers places the average age at 34.2 years with the youngest at eleven and the oldest at 70. Levin and Fox[13] describe the mass murderer as being older than the typical murderer. They state only 15% of mass murderers are under twenty-five, in contrast to 45% of all homicide arrests being under twenty-five.

Profile: Gender

The gender of the mass murder offender is overwhelmingly male. Only five of the 55 mass murderers in Holmes & Holmes[9] were female. In Fessenden's[6] study 93% were male. Douglas and Olshaker[4] describe their typical mass murderer as male. Levin and Fox's[13] sample only one of 42 killers was female.

Profile: Race

The associated race of the mass murder offender is typically white. This is an area where mass murders differ significantly from other murders in the United States. Whereas blacks commit half the homicides in this country, only one in five mass killers is black[13]. The racial composition would seem to more closely approximate that of the population itself. Douglas and Olshaker[4] also infer that the race of the offender is in line with a country's racial makeup.

Profile: Motivation

The motivation of the mass murder is an element crucial in typology. A partial answer lies in the location of the motivation, either intrinsic or extrinsic[9]. With Disciple killers, the motivation is extrinsic as the leader commands an action. The motivation is also extrinsic for the Set-and-

Run Killer, as the desire may be material gain for self or impacting the target's ability to make money. The other three typologies have something intrinsic as their motivation.

Profile: Anticipated Gain

The anticipated gain is another categorization factor. The gains are either psychological or material[9]. All typologies except the Set-and-Run Killer have anticipated gains being psychological. The Set-and-Run Killer, again, has basis in material gain.

Profile: Intelligence and Mental Illness

The intelligence of the mass murderer is a subjective factor. There are often articulate enough to be very comfortable with written communication, expressing their frustration and anger in letters to authorities and newspapers, as well as personal diaries[4]. Many have college degrees, but are unemployed[6]. They seem to have the intelligence to achieve, but have not been able to live up to that expectation. Intelligence does not seem to play as much of a factor as does mental illness in both Disgruntled Workers and Pseudo

Commandos. Fessenden[6] found that more than half of all these type of killers had histories of serious mental health problems, these being identified as hospitalization for mental illness, a prescription for psychiatric drugs, a suicide attempt or evidence of psychosis.

Profile: Spatial Mobility

Spatial mobility is broken into two factors: geographically stable and geographically transient[10]. The Family Annihilator, the Pseudo Commando, and the Disgruntled Employee are typically geographically stable. They kill at or near where they live and/or work. The Disciple and the Set-and-Run Killer are more likely to be geographically transient. The Disciple will typically kill near the location of the leader. The Set-and-Run Killer is likely to include distance from the event as part of the pre-established escape plan[9].

Profile: Victim Traits

Victim traits are not an apparent factor. The victim is typically in the wrong place at the wrong time. As such, victim traits are non-specific for all five typologies[9].

Profile: Victim Relationship and

Selectivity

Victim relationship and victim selectivity is a factor in the Family Annihilator and Disgruntled Employee typologies. The key to the Family Annihilator is killing his family. The Disgruntled Employee goes to his former workplace to kill, murdering those he used to know and work with. For the other typologies the victims are normally strangers and randomly chosen.

Profile: Other Factors

Other factors to consider are precursor behavior or events, firearm ownership, and abuse history. Precursor behavior includes: recent unemployment or a long period of unemployment; loneliness or depression; a family break up; troubles at work, including disciplinary actions; telling people what they are going to do before they commit the mass murder; and writing angry and frustrated letters to newspapers or public officials[14]. Firearm ownership to the point of obsession or recent obtainment of firearms[4] with predominant preference of semiautomatic weapons[6] is common. A history of abuse is also a common theme, either as the victim or the perpetrator[4].

Profile: Suicide Rate

For most of the typologies, suicide or death at the hands of police is the outcome of the mass murder event for the killer[9]. In Fessenden's[6] rampage killer study, 45% either tried to or did commit suicide and another 9% were killed by police. The exceptions are the Disciple, who desires to live on to please the leader, and the Set-and-Run Killer, who plans from the outset to escape.

Increasing Numbers

With apparent increasing frequency, the public is given news via television and print of yet another horrendous crime of mass murder. Wilson and Wilson[15] contend that something has gone wrong in society that mass murder killers are multiplying at a high rate. Fessenden[6] does state the attacks are rare when compared to other American murders, but have provoked intense national discussion on crime, education and American culture. Dietz[2] notes that the definition of mass murder in itself eliminates more than 99% of violent crimes and thus makes mass murder an extremely rare social event.

As the size of the population of the United States grows, so do the overall number of murders. In 1900, the reported number of murders was 230. This is opposed to the reported number of 22,270 for 1989. The rate was 1.2 per 100,000 reported murdered in 1989[8]. So, the overall murder rate for the United States has increased, and with it, so has the rate of multicide.

Subject: Joseph Wesbecker

Background

Joseph "Rocky" Wesbecker was born on April 27, 1942. His father, a construction worker, was killed in a fall in 1943, when Joseph was little more than a year old. He was raised, an only child, by his mother, Martha, with a lot of help from grandma, Nancy Montgomery, and a host of aunts in Louisville, Kentucky[3].

Wesbecker was a moderate student and left high school just as soon as he could. In the prevailing climate of opportunity and prosperity, this did no serious damage to his prospects and by 1960 he had a steady job as a pressman in a printing plant. The following year he got married. The marriage produced two sons, Joseph Jr. and James, but did not last, ending with an acrimonious divorce and a bitter battle over the custody and support arrangements for the children[3].

In 1971, Wesbecker moved to a new job in the printing industry, also in Louisville, with the Standard Gravure Corporation. Standard Gravure, although quite a sizeable outfit, was very much run as a family business and the employees were, for the most part, content in their work and felt themselves to be "part of the family."[3]

Wesbecker married a second time in 1983, but was divorced again just a year later. Wesbecker had a long history of mental and emotional problems. Two marriages ended in divorce. He had been hospitalized on a voluntarily basis at least three times between 1978 for these problems[5].

In marked contrast to Wesbecker's tumultuous personal life, his working life was extremely stable. By 1986, he had spent more than twenty-five years in the printing industry, the last fifteen of them with Standard Gravure. His work record, in what was an otherwise ill-starred life, was one thing about which he could feel justifiably proud[3].

In 1986, though, everything changed when Standard Gravure's owners, the Bingham family, sold up. The new management's priority was to shed any excess fat on the company and to sharpen its teeth and claws, making it fit to fight in the dog-eat-dog economic climate of the day. One of the first things to go was the feeling the employees had that they were part of a family. Their futures were no longer certain[3].

Faced with demands from his company for greater efficiency and productivity, Wesbecker was found wanting, and he sought the help of his union. "Almost from the beginning, on the very first day, he laid it out cold and told me he was a manic depressive and was taking medication," union lawyer Herbert Segal revealed. "Some days he had good days and other times he didn't and talked about conspiracies to harass him."[3] Whereas, previously, Wesbecker's deficiencies had been accommodated with a measure of tolerance and compassion by Standard Gravure, few allowances appear to have been made for him under the new management. Due to the poor performance, Wesbecker's supervisor began giving him poor job performance ratings[9].

Wesbecker became obsessed with the tense labor situation. His grievances with the company encompassed the general: from the relocation of an employees' car parking lot farther from the plant and a ban on the ink-stained pressmen from using the lifts to the administrative offices; to the personal: he had been assigned to running a mechanical folder in the printing of advertising supplements, but felt he could not cope with the precision and timing of the work. He complained of stress and asked to be returned to his old job, operating the ink-running wheels, but his request fell on deaf ears[3]. The change in jobs was actually a promotion, but Wesbecker could not handle the increased stresses. He claimed that his exposure to an industrial chemical had caused memory loss, dizziness, and blackouts. He further attributed to the chemical exposure his bouts of sleeplessness, racing thoughts, anxiety, anger, and confusion[5].

Finally, in May 1987, he lodged a complaint with Louisville's Human Relations Commission, charging that, in view of his mental disability, Standard Gravure had discriminated against him. Commission investigators confirmed that Wesbecker - by this time on sick leave - was a manic-depressive and found reasonable basis for his charge of discrimination. "The rule in discrimination cases involving mental or physical disabilities is that the employer is required to reasonably accommodate the person and the condition," Gwendolyn Young, the executive director of the Human Relations Commission, explained. "As far as we know, the company, without admitting discrimination, agreed to return him to his old position when he was well enough to come back to work."[3]

In the three years following the takeover of Standard Gravure, Wesbecker's work for the company became increasingly sporadic and his outlook was increasingly bitter. A police officer that knew him said that in these latter years he became "argumentative and confrontational."[3] Relatives said he attempted suicide on three occasions[1].

Wesbecker often had articulated his feelings of worthlessness and had in fact attempted suicide on three occasions, once though a drug overdose, another by breathing car exhaust fumes, and a third by hanging. He further articulated a desire to harm others in addition to his suicide attempts. Fellow employees recalled his conversations surrounding his fantasies of revenge against his company should he be mistreated[5].

In 1989, Wesbecker was placed on long-term disability leave and his bitterness towards the company grew. "They done him dirty," his aunt, Mildred Higgins told the Louisville Courier-Journal (1989). Colleagues knew that Wesbecker "talked about coming back and wiping the place out and how he was going to get even with the company."[3]

Apparently no one in Wesbecker's family knew of his longstanding fascination with guns. A snub-nose .38-calibre revolver, bought from a Memphis dealer in 1974, was probably the first of the many firearms he purchased. Over the years, the collection grew to include a Colt 6-mm revolver, a shotgun and a .32-calibre revolver[3].

In August 1988, he began adding semi-automatic weapons to his arsenal. His first purchase was a SIG-Sauer 9-mm pistol. In February 1989, he also bought two MAC-11 pistols. Jack Tilford, a gunshop owner, recalled telling him that the MAC-11 cost $249. Wesbecker replied, "At that price, I want two." In May, he returned to Tilford's store to buy an AK-47 rifle. Tilford asked him how he liked the MAC-11 and Wesbecker said he loved it. He told Tilford on each visit that he wanted the guns for target shooting. He had a valid firearms purchase permit and, so far as Tilford could tell, "He was normal in every way."[12].

In the summer of 1989, Nancy Montgomery, the grandmother who had helped raise Wesbecker, died. By early September, though, his mind was focused back on the situation at Standard Gravure. According to his Aunt Mildred, "He was upset about things at work and said they will get paid back. He said things like that all the time, and I would agree with him and just listen. You know, it was just a figure of speech."[11].

A psychiatrist's notes show that Joseph Wesbecker rejected the doctor's suggestion to enter a hospital three days before Wesbecker went on a killing rampage at Standard Gravure Corp. in downtown Louisville. Dr. Lee A. Coleman's records show that, during a Sept. 11 session, Wesbecker wept and exhibited "tangential thought" and "increased level of agitation and anger."[7]

The Event

At 8:30 A.M. on 14 September 1989, Wesbecker arrived at the Standard Gravure plant carrying a duffel bag containing an

AK-47 semiautomatic assault rifle, two MAC-11 semiautomatic pistols, a 9mm semiautomatic pistol, and a .38-caliber revolver. He carried hundreds of rounds of ammunition. When encountering a friend, John Tingle, who tried to persuade Wesbecker not to enter the plant, Wesbecker ordered Tingle to "get away," stating, "I told them that I'd be back."[3]. None of the workers in the vicinity was about to argue. They retreated to a cloakroom and locked the door. On that morning, Wesbecker walked into the Standard Gravure plant, intent on seeking revenge on those who he perceived as the cause of his problems[3].

After he gained entry to the plant, Wesbecker went seeking out the executive office complex. Wesbecker took the elevator, in petty defiance of company rules, to the third floor administrative offices. He opened fire as the elevator door parted, killing the receptionist and wounding several others of the office staff. Tingle speculated: "He was up there looking for bosses. He couldn't find the bosses and couldn't find the supervisors. He was just in too deep to turn back. So he just shot anything that was close to him."[3]. As he did so, he worked his way back downstairs. In the snack bar, he fired copper-cased 7.62-mm bullets from the AK-

47 rifle into a refrigerator, a vending machine, and into one of the seven people who died during the rampage. He then proceeded down the hallway to the bindery, spraying the area with gunfire and killing and wounding more plant employees. He then moved to the Courier-Journal building, where he shot another employee.[11].

Wesbecker proceeded to the Standard Gravure pressroom, into the basement, and back to the pressroom, firing his weapon all the way until he dropped his AK-47, raised his SIG-Sauer 9mm pistol under his chin, and killed himself. All events occurred within approximately nine minutes from the firing of the first shot. The police arrived on the scene, finding Wesbecker dead. It was determined that he had fired hundreds of shots during his random murder spree[3].

When police arrived, a worker sitting in a chair, bleeding from a stomach wound, pointed grimly at Wesbecker's body sprawled on the floor, a few yards away. On or close by the body, police found, in addition to the SIG-Sauer and the AK-47 rifle, Wesbecker's two MAC-11 semi-automatic pistols, the snub-nose.38, a bayonet and hundreds of rounds of ammunition. Standard Gravure employee Joe White told reporters, "This guy's been talking about this for a year. He's been talking about guns and Soldier of Fortune magazine. He's paranoid and he thought everyone was after him."[3].

Wesbecker's victims were all secondary targets because the primary targets of his aggression were the company's administrators, who were not found in their offices at the time of the assault. His victims were fellow employees, yet Wesbecker considered them to be enemies for that particular day because they symbolized the organizational structure of Standard Gravure[5].

One survivor of the killings stated that when he heard what were simply loud and unusual sounds, remarked, "I bet that's crazy Joe Wesbecker coming back to kill us all." (Yates, 1992). Little did he suspect, until later, the level of carnage. Wesbecker killed seven persons and wounded thirteen others, most with multiple gunshot wounds, one with a heart attack[5].

Joseph T. Wesbecker, a twice-divorced, forty-seven-year-old, white male, had asked for a transfer from his job as a pressman. He had complained that the job was too stressful, and as his emotional problems worsened during February 1989, his employers responded by placing him on disability leave. Wesbecker felt his employers at Standard Gravure Corporation had inflicted a gross injustice upon him, despite the fact that in reality, his extreme behavior interfered with his duties and the duties of others in his workplace. Nearly every day for seven months, he brooded over how he would repay those in authority who were responsible for his alleged mistreatment.

Profile

Wesbecker's feelings and acts of isolation, withdrawal, and depression are all prominent pre-offense behavior dynamics of the mass and spree authority killer. Further, he was a single, middle-aged, white male, who harbored a long-term grudge against the management of his employer and had accompanying emotional problems relating to his personal work related life. Wesbecker often spoke of his deep resentment toward his employer. Fellow employees recalled his conversations surrounding his fantasies of revenge against his company should he be mistreated.

Wesbecker often had articulated his feelings of worthlessness and had attempted suicide on three occasions, once though a drug overdose, another by breathing car exhaust fumes, and a third by hanging. He further articulated a desire to harm others in addition to his suicide attempts. The investigation failed to link Wesbecker with any of his victims in terms of a personal cause or motive for shooting or killing any one or all of the individuals. Therefore, it must be assumed the shootings were random in nature, rather than specific.

This crime is classified as a mass type of authority killing in that it was a confrontational assault spread throughout a large area (several buildings), leaving many dead and wounded in the wake of the assailant. Wesbecker, during approximately nine minutes, killed seven people and wounded twelve others. He obviously intended to kill all who crossed his path and was intent on revenge, seeking out those of authority in the company for which he worked. The offender came to the scene with multiple weapons and an abundance of ammunition. His shots were intended to be lethal, as demonstrated by the death toll and the fact that of the twelve surviving victims, five were critically wounded. Wesbecker was very mission oriented with no escape plan.

Forensic Findings

Seven dead and twelve wounded people were found at the scene by police authorities. Another victim died three days later. Most of the victims died from massive blood loss due to gunshot wounds to the heart and chest area. Most of the twelve wounded workers were in serious to critical condition.

Typology

Joseph Westbecker fits the typology of the Disgruntled Worker. He returned to his former place of employment and killed seven former coworkers and wounded thirteen more. He was 47 years old when he went on his rampage, which fits the profile. He was also a White male.

His motivation was intrinsic, which fits the profile. Wesbecker returned to his former place of employment to make the bosses pay for what he perceived they had done to him. He wanted them to pay for his suffering.

His anticipated gain was psychological. This fits the profile. Wesbecker wanted to know in his mind that they paid with their lives for destroying his life. Though he did take many lives, he missed his intended targets of the supervisory staff.

Here is a case where intelligence is a subjective matter. Wesbecker was not a stupid man, nor was he overly intelligent. He did not have a college degree. He was unemployed, but that had to do with being placed on disability for his mental illness. So not living up to an expectation created by intelligence, greed, and ambition was not a factor as it is in other types of mass murder. Wesbecker just wanted to keep what he had, which he could not due to his mental issues. His job defined who he was and that was taken away. He blamed the company for their actions and acted out against them. Here, intelligence was not the factor, but instead it was mental illness. Wesbecker was on a host of psychiatric medications and had a history of multiple suicide attempts. Wesbecker felt his employers at Standard Gravure Corporation had inflicted a gross injustice upon him, despite the fact that in reality, his extreme behavior interfered with his duties and the duties of others in his workplace. Nearly every day for seven months, he brooded over how he would repay those in authority who were responsible for his alleged mistreatment.

Wesbecker also fits the profile for spatial mobility. He was geographically stable. He committed his crime at his former place of work, which was near his home. He had no interest in escaping afterward, so that type of transience is not a factor.

Victim traits were not a factor, which is part of the profile. In fitting with the profile, victim relationship and victim selectivity were factors. He had a relationship to the victims from the aspect that he used to work with them and knew them. They were not strangers. Wesbecker went to the factory with the intention of targeting his former supervisors. The investigation failed to link Wesbecker with any of his victims in terms of a personal cause or motive for shooting or killing any one or all of the individuals. Therefore, it must be assumed the shootings were random in nature, rather than specific. Unable to kill the supervisors, he shot anyone who was there.

Other factors in the profile to consider are precursor behaviors, firearm ownership, and abuse history. Wesbecker had extensive precursor behavior, which included: losing his job by being placed on disability; Wesbecker's feelings and acts of isolation, withdrawal, and depression are all prominent pre-offense behavior dynamics; he had multiple divorces; he had gotten poor performance appraisals from his supervisor prior to being placed on disability; he commented to many people, both coworkers and family, on his desire to make the company pay through violence; he had filed a grievance with the Louisville Human Relations Commission against his employer for discriminating against him due to his mental disability, which he won. Wesbecker had a history of obsession with firearms, especially semi-automatic weapons. He had made a point of purchasing several of the then recently outlawed assault type weapons. Wesbecker had a rather unremarkable childhood, with no reported history of abuse. This one factor does not fit the profile.

Wesbecker definitely fit the profile for being suicidal. He made no plan for escape. He took his life at the scene of the murders at the conclusion of his rampage.

Profile Summary

Wesbecker fit well with the mass murder typology of Disgruntled Worker, meeting fifteen of the sixteen profile characteristics. He met the statistical expectations for age, gender (male), race (white), motivation (intrinsic to make "them" pay), gain (intrinsic), intelligence (moderate), spatial mobility (at work near his home), victim traits (targeted), victim relationship (former coworkers), victim selectivity (targeted), precursor behavior (based around resentment), firearm ownership (yes) mental health (on disability for it) and suicidal ideation. He did not meet the criteria for abuse history, as none was reported.

Psychiatric History and Medication Factor

Psychiatric history

Wesbecker had a long history of psychiatric illness and was treated for it in hospitals at least three times between 1978 and 1987. He was diagnosed as suffering from alternating episodes of deep depression and manic depression. He had episodes of confusion, anger and anxiety and made several attempts to commit suicide.

Hospital records also suggested that Wesbecker posed a threat to himself and others.

According to CBS's 60 Minutes, "In 1984, five years before he took Prozac, Wesbecker's medical records show that he had this conversation with a doctor. Have you ever felt like harming someone else? 'Yes,' Wesbecker said. Who? 'My foreman.' When? 'At work.' The same medical records show Wesbecker had already attempted suicide 12 to 15 times."

In the years prior to the shooting, Wesbecker more than once threatened to "kill a bunch of people" or to bomb Standard Gravure. A one point, he even considered hiring an assassin to kill several executives of the company. Apparently he even discussed these things with his wife before their divorce. When he left Standard Gravure in August 1988, he told other workers that he would come back, wipe out the place and get even with the company. Shortly before the shooting, he told one of his aunts that he was upset about things at work and said they will get paid back, but as he said these things all the time, she didn't take the threat too seriously.

One of the employees at Standard Gravure said after the shooting: "This guy's been talking about this for a year. He's been talking about guns and Soldier of Fortune magazine. He's paranoid, and he thought everyone was after him."

Three days prior to the shooting, on September 11, Wesbecker told his psychiatrist that a foreman had forced Wesbecker to perform oral sex on him in front of his co-workers to get off the folder equipment he was assigned to be operating. In his notes, the psychiatrist wrote "Prozac?"

Medication Lawsuit

In the early 1990's, Dr. PeterBreggin was selected to be the scientific and medical expert for all of the more than 100 combined Prozac-related cases brought against the manufacturer, Eli Lilly and Company (makers of Prozac®). Dr. Breggin was tasked to evaluate for the plaintiffs the scientific basis for the claim that Prozac was causing violence and suicide, and also to evaluate the drug company's potential negligence in the development and marketing of Prozac. This was including any attempts to hide the risk of Prozacinduced suicide and violence. He was also asked to evaluate individual cases for their merit.

Survivors and relatives of the dead in Wesbecker's rampage took Lilly to court in 1994. They claimed that Wesbecker's violence was due to Prozac.
In the process of serving as the expert medical witness in this case, Dr. Breggin evaluated and testified about a number of key documents. At first, the trial was apparently won by Eli Lilly. The jury found that Prozac was not at fault. However, the judge later determined that the trial had been rigged. Eli Lilly had paid the plaintiffs to throw the trial by withholding damaging evidence against the company. Dr. Breggin describes his participation in this dramatic case in detail in his latest book, *Medication Madness* (July 2008).

For many years after the fixed trial, plaintiffs, attorneys and even the FDA remained unaware of many of the documents Breggin had discovered and/or evaluated. Then in 2004, an anonymous individual sent the documents to the *British Medical Journal* (BMJ), who published an article about them and also distributed them. When Eli Lilly forced the BMJ to apologize for suggesting that the documents had "disappeared" while in Eli

Lilly's care, Breggin wrote an unpublished letter to BMJ explaining how the documents had indeed disappeared. Though criticizing BMJ for saying that the company had in effect hidden the smoking guns, Eli Lilly never actually contested the allegations surrounding the documents in that the drug company had withheld evidence that Prozac caused suicide.

Evaluation

Rocky Wesbecker was an angry man. His extensive history of mental illness bred an unwavering paranoia and rage in him for every perceived slight or injustice against him, especially from his employer. He also had a pattern of suicidal ideation. It was very likely that he was in a great deal of emotional and physical pain. The combination of these factors came to a head when he felt the pain was too much to bear any more and those that he felt caused it needed to pay before he ended his pain. Did psychiatric medications play a part in this? Possibly, but perhaps he was already standing on the precipice just needing a small push.

References

1. Cramer, C. (1993, Winter). Ethical problems of mass murder coverage in the mass media. <u>Journal of Mass Media Ethics, 9</u>(1), 26-42.

2. Dietz, P.E. (1986). Mass, serial and sensational homicides. <u>Bulletin of the New York Academy of Medicine, 62</u>(5),.477-491.

3. Disturbed past of killer of 7 is unraveled. (1989, September 15). <u>Lexington Herald-Leader,</u> A1-A3.

4. Douglas, J., & Olshaker, M. (1999). <u>The anatomy of motive.</u> New York: Scribner.

5. Douglas, J.E., Burgess, A.W., Burgess, A.G., & Ressler, R.F. (1992). <u>Crime classification manuals: A standard system for investigating and classifying violent crimes.</u> San Francisco: Jossey-Bass.

6. Fessenden, F. (2000, April 9). <u>Rampage killers: A statistical portrait. New York Times,</u> A1, A28.

7. Gunman refused to go to hospital 3 days before rampage. (1989, October 27). <u>Lexington Herald-Leader,</u> A1.

8. Harrison, M., & Gilbert, S. (eds) (1996). <u>The murder reference: Everything you never wanted to know about murder in America.</u> San Diego: Excellent Books.

9. Holmes, R.M., & Holmes, S.T. (1992, March). Understanding mass murder: A starting point. <u>Federal Probation, 56(1),</u> 53-61.

10.   Holmes, R.M., & Holmes, S.T. (1996). <u>Profiling violent crime: An investigative tool.</u> Thousand Oaks: Sage Publications.

11.   I want the boss. (1989, September 14). <u>Louisville Courier-Journal,</u> A1.

12.   Killer denied having mental problems, rifle seller says. (1989, September 16). <u>Boston Globe,</u> A1.

13.   Levin, J., & Fox, J.A. (1985). <u>Mass murder: America's growing menace.</u> New York: Plenum Press.

14.   Mendoza, A. (2000). <u>The mass murderer hit list.</u> [Online]. Available: Wysiwyg://21/http://www.mayhem.net/Crime/murder1.html

15.   Wilson, C. & Wilson, D. (1995). <u>The killers among us, book II: Sex, madness and mass murder.</u> New York: Warner Books.

This book is dedicated to my father.

Disclaimer:

The information contained in this book is for informational and entertainment purposes only. Some of the crimes depicted in this book are graphic and not appropriate or intended for those sensitive to such information. If you do not want to be exposed to potentially offensive language or graphic crimes, read no further.

This book details the author's opinions about crimes, criminal behavior and the criminal justice system. The author, though employed in the criminal justice profession and having received education and training in profiling, is not employed as a profiler. The author is not licensed as an attorney and the information is not represented as legal advice. The thoughts and opinions of the author are purely his own and do not represent the opinions of any agency or entity within the criminal justice system.

Except as specifically stated in this book, neither the author or publisher, nor any authors, contributors, or other representatives will be liable for damages arising out of or in connection with the use of this book. This is a comprehensive limitation of liability that applies to all damages of any kind, including (without limitation) compensatory; direct, indirect or consequential damages; loss of data, income or profit; loss of or damage to property and claims of third parties.

The material in this book may include information, products or services by third parties. Third Party Materials comprise of the products and opinions expressed by their owners. As such, I do not assume responsibility or liability for any Third Party material or opinions. The publication of such Third Party Materials does not constitute my guarantee of any information, instruction, opinion, products or services contained within the Third Party Material.

Acknowledgements:

I would like to make formal acknowledgements of the people who have inspired, mentored, motivated and helped me over the years. But, the circumstances that require my anonymity prohibit that. I am still grateful.

I am currently working on projects related the time I have spent in probation.   I am also working on other criminal justice topics related to true crime.

A lot of time and effort took place in not only writing each of the reports included in this book, but in the creation of the book itself. Please to not share or distribute without permission, but instead refer others to the website to purchase their own copy.

Please take the time to review this book from the site you purchased it from!! I do read it and appreciate the feedback. Like any author, I do enjoy hearing from those who enjoyed the book!

I can be contacted (and followed) at the

following locations:

My blog:
http://probationuncovered.blogspot.com/

Facebook:
https://www.facebook.com/probationuncove
red

Twitter: @PODoe2015

Email: probationuncovered@gmail.com

Probation Titles Available from this Author:

Maximum Exposure: 42 Stories from Probation
http://amzn.com/B013NUJ8NS

Newbie Status: A Guide for Probation Officers to Navigate their First Five Years and Beyond
http://amzn.com/B014NF1EQ6

Left on Vacation Came Home on Probation: A Guide to Successfully Completing your Probation
http://amzn.com/B013N8T2YU

Gang Conditions: A Guide to Supervising Gang Members on Probation
http://amzn.com/B013N7D8BY

Sustained: Probation Internal Affairs Investigations and Your Rights
http://a.co/0wZJ0jw

On The Stand: Courtroom Testimony for Probation Officers
http://a.co/fagRuBQ

Just the Facts: Report Writing for Probation Officers
http://a.co/23InJpl

Fifteen 15 Minute Training Topics: Quick Training Topics for Probation Officers (Probation Training Topics)
http://a.co/1wEG43K

True Crime Titles Available from this Author:

The Woodchipper Murder: The Forensic Evidence Trail in the Homicide of Helle Crafts
http://amzn.com/B013N6DYDM

Set and Run: A Profile of Timothy McVeigh
http://amzn.com/B015F9S908

96 Minutes of Hell: Shots from the Tower
http://amzn.com/B013N8BCIO

Disciple or Partner: A Profile of Charles "Tex" Watson
http://amzn.com/B0163JNEEK

Disgruntled or Over-Medicated: A Profile of Joseph Wesbecker
http://amzn.com/B01652QUGY

Annihilator: A Profile of John List
http://amzn.com/B0163WTU54

The Killing Frenzy: Profiling Mass Murder
http://amzn.com/B0163JZG0U

Messy Murders: Death and Dismemberment by Chainsaw
http://a.co/d/9msk9Ok